www.finishinglinepress.com

Moods of the Dream Fog

poems by

Wendy Gist

Finishing Line Press
Georgetown, Kentucky

Moods of the Dream Fog

ACKNOWLEDGMENTS

Grateful acknowledgment is made to the editors of the publications where individual
poems have appeared.

Burningword—"Visitor at Tsaile Lake," "Fragments of Southwestern Youth"
Canyon Voices—"Unspoken"
Empty Mirror—"Winter Walk at Nightfall"
Gravel—"Four Absolutes"
Grey Sparrow Journal—"Reaping the Whirlwind," "Upon Discovering Desert Canoeing," "Bosque
Reclamation"
Juked—"Pollywogs"
Lines + Stars—"I-10 East Near Las Cruces, New Mexico"
Pif Magazine—"Canyon de Chelly Echoes"
Poetry Pacific—"Passion Fog." "The Stirring"
Red Booth Review—"Humpty Dumpty Deli"
Soundings Review—"Midsummer Night at Isotopes Park"
Sundog Lit—"Dodging the Super Bowl"
The Chaffey Review—"Cuke & Halo"
The Fourth River—"Morning Beat"
The Galway Review—"To My Dream," "Intimate Waters," "Blush"
Yellow Medicine Review—"Drip Wish"

Publisher: Leah Maines

Editor: Christen Kincaid

Cover Art: Allen Forrest

Author Photo: John Gist

Cover Design: Elizabeth Maines

Printed in the USA on acid-free paper.
Order online: www.finishinglinepress.com
               also available on amazon.com

Author inquiries and mail orders:
Finishing Line Press
P. O. Box 1626
Georgetown, Kentucky 40324
U. S. A.

Table of Contents

1

*Shades
of
Red*

To My Dream

*"Dreams are true while they last,
and do we not live in dreams?"*
—*Alfred Lord Tennyson*

It's electrifying the way in which
we collide: your mouth wants I.

Time is nonexistent. The dream
begins and you dowse me.

I know nothing about
a dream's needs—only a sheen

like an ocean of stars.
My god, come here.

No, don't let me see;
I'm at the outer edge of that realm.

If you vanish—would I know
your odor? And, if so,

would these reveries be unreal,
forgotten, surreal, and the chance

of another lucid moment,
nothing more than phantasm?

Electrolysis of Love
(for my husband)

Your pupils dilate
as you take away

eye-glasses; blink, blink, beam.
You must surely guess,

but I'll confess: you penetrate
deep within the salty sea of me.

How do you impart such mastery
in morning minutes of you and I

to halt a breath?
Surrender your hot heart,

lips, hair, airs...
Your ebb and flow possess

ability to remove self from thyself.
I want to do to you

what moon lilies do by night.

Winter Walk at Nightfall
(for my husband)

I want to walk with you
bundled under snowflakes at nightfall.
I will cook hot soup—

Lentil, chicken noodle
any kind.
I will brew hot tea—

Earl Grey, jasmine
whatever you desire,
pour heat into thermos to-go.

Let me walk with you awhile
out to the winter woods.
We can break for a meal

and watch the snow
tumble tumble like stardust
through the still winter night.
.
Let me press tender
my thirsted-for flesh
to your

moon-lit lips
as our hearts dissolve in union.
As for me, let me see

and feel the warm life
in your lovesick breath
steaming mysterious across the air.

Intimate Waters
(for John)

If you want me
I'll be in the foam of timeless now

silent as a ghost
in love with the living.

Come find me there,
and part my Red Sea

with your tonic of stars
that elevate the light.

Merge our intimate waters
in a spume of mystery.

Blush

(for John)

You can touch flesh
with your gentle fingers
darker than my bright body

transparent as a tear

that drips from an icicle
passing through in the sun
shaft of a New Year's afternoon:

your sinewy hands may knead
tummy, birthmarks, fondle all nakedness
matchless as a single snowflake.

You can witness my neck, breast,
belly, knees and toes
blush carnations presented to you

in this ritual of breath.

Cuke & Halo

Open refrigerator door:

"Cu-cum-ber calling,"
She'd say. "Let's have a little…
Crunch of cuke."
Cool air smacks veiny shins
At undone hem of
Fuchsia mumu.

Close refrigerator door:

Spread brown bread slices with newfangled
 Miracle Whip Light.
 "Or bread un-spread will do," she'd say.
"To taste Ezekiel a bit better."
Crack of pepper.

Open sliding door:

Noontime, two triangles each
Of cucumber sandwich treats.
Grandmother's sponge-roller hair haloed pink
Against California rose garden. Balmy, fragrant, 68-degrees.
Leg warmers dangle from rattan chair,
Miniskirt ruffle neon pink, I'm a
Valley girl for a week.

Open refrigerator door once more:

Smithereens of hair going glittery grey,
I hear the whisper inside, though she's
Gone from this world:
"Cu-cum-ber calling. Let's have a little…
Crunch of cuke."

Arizona rose rock. Arid, fragrant, 68-degrees.
Pink rose petals float from my mind
To fill the fridge:
A dozen pink roses in an urn,
Cuke & halo, as if to say,
"Triangles prove heaven."

2

*Shades
of
Yellow*

Midsummer Night at Isotopes Park

"I see great things in baseball. It's our game—the American game."
—Walt Whitman

Now patrons face the field bedizened by ads, distant flags—
New Mexico, United States, P.O.W—flapping. We relax on box
seats between 3rd and home. Sugar-strewn summery dusk.

Sacramento River Cats vs. Albuquerque Isotopes.
Floodlights beam the action as retro night blares '80s songs.
Moth wings of evening flurry, while a carousal glows into the dark

backdrop of the park's kid zone like a UFO sitting on the peak
of Sandia Mountains. And beneath the fun, blankets sprawl fans
melting at Creamland Berm. Right fielder River Cat paces in heat.

Swing. Whack. 2 runs score. 3 to 0. Whistles and claps. Bottom
of the 4th. The crowd chows giant cookies, kettle corn, foot-long
corndogs, dripping tortilla burgers, green chile dogs, funnel cake fries.

Fine men I so love, husband and son, grub nachos, imbibe
pricey beer. Fun-loving women fork strawberries and kiwis
from fruit cups, sip Blue Moon draft, turn tipsy to us, laugh,

"Will you catch the speeding ball when it flies?" 7th inning stretch.
Palms to hearts: God Bless America. Youth in chile suits run red
and green pepper race, red takes the lead. All the way.

And now EMT's aid a man four rows down. Murmurs
of heart attack. Cat thwacks home run: 7 to 7. He taunts Isotope's
dugout as he joys on home. Boos ululate the flouncing crowd.

Bullpen empties onto green field, yellow smears of Isotope
jerseys aim to slide-in to the would-be brawl. The struggle
concludes bloodless as cloud cover harbingers thunder.

I-10 East Near Las Cruces, New Mexico
(Late October)

Billboard:
Akela Flats Trading Post.

Two out-of-state cars
exit for expensive gas, and, tempted,
buy junk—snakeskin earrings,
fudge or
maybe a glass scorpion.

Bugs splash on windshield.
Locals on radio broadcast
a longing for first frost
before the next song: Monster Mash.
RV hauls ebony Hummer,

and here now goes big rigs
churning out stinking vapors,
and a vintage turquoise
Cadillac Coupe de Ville
sparkling a yellow license plate.

Up ahead a flutter of birds helix
over yellow painted lines
back to orange-ing desert.

Border Patrol inspection,
cameras aimed at oncoming traffic,
cameras, cameras, cameras.
Ginormous roadrunner perches atop
rest stop hill,
sculpted from recycled trash.

Pecan orchard, the stench of sewer:
Almost there. At last!

Passion Fog

Disintegrate external talk
into tactile trance.

No need to say
anything anymore.

Misty pull: adored gent's
playful sentiment, analgesic.

He piques her:
amatory animal gaze, soft

smile, with a carnal 'umm'
at the back of tongue.

Way too damn fine,
he throbs in a nebulous haze.

She craves his breath
at jugular, ear,

but capture it not
upon the teary December fog.

She can't tell, up till now,
if he strives to bite

or kiss tender.

Dodging the Super Bowl

Striding by a shrine of Mother
Mary perched on brown turf,
I stumble upon a cow skull bone,
then a plastic swan spilling pink
synthetic rosebuds pale.

As I scramble by, hollers girt
the open garage as
youth-full males
boozing too soon roar:
"Go Ravens!"

Deliciousness
from within stucco walls coaxes
the neighborhood, gusto
for good chile bowl green
in dead of winter.

A single raven feather floats
above tip-tops
of knurled trees
flanking the town's
High School football field;

church doors burst vowels
circumnavigating streets
bathed in faith.
And on these concrete strolls
stand strangers in worlds alone:

longwinded conversations
with ghosts,
on sidewalks made
in another age—splitting.

Doves cry
unto the rare moist air
in a border town nicknamed in
1881 New Chicago, where now
prickly pear pads drop to sandy alleys
like green gibbous moons

sprouting spikes that hurt.
Turn to the stark park alight
in wintry sun, soiled earloops
of surgeon's mask dangling
from the chain-link fence and

church bells boom,
sirens shrill, and rounding
the hospital I spy an old man
and his wide grin, watering
a yard of fine grain sand.

He says with a wink of immense
portent, raising the nose of the hose,
trigger pulled,
"When the wind blitz through, water
glues the dirt so it won't fill my yurt."

He lobs white bread stale
to balmy doves
on the sidewalk old
and fractured in front of him,
zigzagging my rush to home.

Humpty Dumpty Deli

Humpty Dumpty dude jots orders with flamingo pen,
scoops rocky road and mango ice cream for tweens
who scream preceding soccer practice.

Humpty places waffle cones oozing melting mounds
into holders on the countertop near antique register,
accepts cash only. An older couple off the Interstate
step forward on tanned legs in Bermuda shorts plaid.

The woman under white visor orders a pistachio shake.
Her hubby in button-down shirt pink, masquerading as boyfriend,
chooses berry banana split, demands in southern twang,
"No cherry, Sir."

A young woman with a parted fro leaps forward,
her asymmetrical skirt, twirling yellow as sun flow.
Tap tap acrylic nail to laminated photo of frappé on countertop.

We chill at blue-mint booths.
He comes to us as waiter, delivers tropical smoothie
and orange Crush pop in a bottle, chilled.
He waggles behind counter, washes knives in a sink,
wipes equipment sterile. Mops tile.

Efficient as fish fins in water. He comes twice as server,
delivers ice waters as if a mind reader and
lunch with a clank of condiments (without request).

We'd slam a $100.00 tip on the table if able. Why not?
It's a sweltering 103 degrees out. Heck.
We go, stroll sidewalks, flip-flops melt soles.
Humpty's up on the rooftop mending the air conditioner.
If he goes tumbling, who will bus the tables?

Upon Discovering Desert Canoeing

In an alcove of tuff rock
I sit in stillness
skin exfoliated by wind
and watch out a blue air arch.

So see what I see
is a light-flecked desert:
lamps of the lord yucca shining
among cow's tongue cacti.

The flowerheads
ooze creamy petals
wilting atop slender bodies
like candlewax melting

where there are no
streams or lakes
not even an oasis
of which I know.

And I am mindful
of light sublime
as a sun-lathered nomad
slips into my mirage

waving a snake stick
like a magic trick.
And now roving down
the curving road

mansions on wheels too
high and wide and long
swallow the drifter
in currents of dirt.
Hummers follow

in rapids of dust
carrying clasped canoes
the color of poppies and white-gold
on polished roofs.

In a dark stone pocket
at my thumb, not a trace
of April showers.
In this ritual of stillness

I have never seen
such a splash among yuccas
and imagine the RV drivers
like children in sandboxes

wild with toys
wedged in shallows of grit:
under failing light
oars pummel dry earth

as if it were the water of life.

Bosque Reclamation

And today, pastels
smudge the Bosque.
Early light
saddles distant mesas.
Native grasses
kink towards foothills,
in a clean breeze,
line the marbled waters:
peach, lilac, pink, green.

Naturalist Jill,
discovers feathers here
and there
and rabbit scat in sand, some
zygodactyl feet scrawling
sideways and back:
reclaimed country tells
the old story.

She steps
up to boardwalk,
leans over guardrail,
binocs hanging
from her
ostrich neck,
the water current weaving
like a loose braid
below.

Snowy
egret hunted
for vintage vanity
in 19th century:
No more shaggy feathers
in the dear ladies' caps,
whisper her lips
on the clear wind.

Breath
of chill morning,
Jill faces mirror
of self,
in water,
hears duck dabble,
and song from folds
of shadow, shore birds
restored scientific.

She lifts looking glass
to eye a Canada goose,
slow motion swivel, optic zoom:
built-in wetland:
finds a visible bird
preening on a snag:
streaked breast inflated unnatural:
Cooper's hawk.

Cottonwood branches
reach up and out,
trill leaves anew.
Deer move through
refuge fields
of indigo hues
to slake thirst
from Rio Grande.

Yet, a great blue heron,
still,
eyes Jill near
the bank,
waits to spear a frog or fish:
windswept chest-plume tasseling
beneath
the bill that kills.

3

*Shades
of
Blue*

Four Absolutes

It's a nuclear afternoon.

An old lady
standing in the pharmacy line
sobs: "I already know
what they're going to tell me."

You dab sweat from temples,
plead to God you don't black out,
steer your mind to a bath at home, chamomile tinged.

Mortality mutters triumphant.
The urge to flee builds like an overfull bladder.

A display of artificial tulips near racks of allergy pills
bouquets electric yellow.

The doctor told you there are four absolutes:
alive; dead; pregnant; not pregnant.

At home, knowing there is no cure,
you swallow what he prescribed.

Water flows, fills the tub.

Reaping the Whirlwind

These are the days leading to your forty-fourth
b-day: spinning in an allergic spell. Elements of place
where your head about goes faint rapt in sky-
blazed filth cloud the color of jicama skin. This
is how your birth month roils with grains.
The deadly blendings turn you light-headed
and leave you breathing dust, gasping, yet
you've got a prescribed Epi-pen ready to needle.
Ragweed, juniper, mesquite, chile pepper farm
insecticides, creosote, borderlands
sand, forest-fire smoke from miles away,
and who knows what more soars
in this spring aridity: 2 % humidity. Whistling
in through the rattling window, dust seeps
and leaches its way through every old house. Out
the dog-slobbered glass you see trees
shaking at the street corner, a St. Vitus Dance
choreographed by gods of disorder. Glossy new
mulberry leaves sparkle in the bright light
like quivering peridot gemstones
offering some holy promise. One limb
snaps and somersaults and twists and
tics onto the sidewalk and into the street. The
humidifier blurps beneath your stuffy head
as you lie frozen on the sofa frozen
'til the swelling subsides (you so pray)
staring at the apricot walls up to the light
fixture centered on the ceiling above
coiled in pretty brass leaves. Who could
believe you hear the neighbor's weed-eater
in such windswept upheaval? Coming
and going like a gigantic fly at your ear,

weeds fly and ribbon in the anxious air
and your heart skips two beats. After clicking
the radio remote to the yoga healing station,
your pulse returns to normal
and you imagine yourself drifting
through tomorrow's unadulterated clouds
floating to forever, a place dreamed but yet to be revealed.

Pollywogs

The pond morphs pollywogs
the size of babies' fists

some with

legs

some with

arms

some with

both (arms & legs)

all with

tails

to paddle water's edge
to intermingle with sprawling sweet peas.

& I lean my heart
toward bountiful bullfrogs,

their peeping bulge eyes
protruding from clods of moss,

& note:
the water a fiery green.

& frozen in water's mossy womb,
a lone frog bloats.

The Stirring

Girls nosh mangoes
sold on sticks
in plain air.
They relish the dance before them:
red & yellow in a row,
skirts spinning
allergic swirl of pollen mesquite.
They watch mariachi from concrete
bleachers, arid breeze echoes
clapping applause,
unaware of dirt
devils, dust devils, the dirt
stirring behind them.

4

*Shades
of
Green*

Morning Beat

> *"Nobody sees a flower really; it is so small. We haven't time, and to see takes time—like to have a friend takes time."* —*Georgia O'Keeffe*

North

Buttery sunshine spreads smooth over juniper dabbed dirt. Blue heron plunges from pine fluff, skims lake green as gunpowder tea. Shores smell of moss, dead carp, of stink-bait. Light exposes an orgy of insects, glints the bustle like an unearthly galaxy of eye-level stars: black butterflies, bluebottle fly wings. Ensy-teensy helicopter dragonflies hover black and white as law books, the buzzing beauties tinkle noses, orbit human skulls. The way: Indian paintbrush, wild morning glory, New Mexico thistle, buckhorn cholla. Lichen-coated rocks dry we mount, footfall down, up, look, oh: "There's a dragonfly orange as habanero." Mud hen carves a V that changes to I back to M bold, dunks under green water. Vim.

East

Bull frogs hear our spongy steps near, trombone a warning, plop to mud puddling, slick slide against trim cattail reeds that rise high above our straw brim hats. Sacred datura's trumpet petals close up all swirly and pearly like one-of-a-kind art blown glass. We human hikers tuck under caterpillar tents out to black crawlies on grains dispersed in surfeit of cowboy toilet paper plants. No cell phone signals here. One must have faith in mullein to shoo evils away. Does one dare disconnect to connect? Path deviates through weeds that scratch shoulders raw, that bleeds out to a patch of stinging nettles. I've never seen so many prickly poppies crinkle in godly light like torn pieces of crepe wedding streamers rumpling back into yolk dank hearts. A rafter of turkeys wobbles horizontal, forms a cross.

South

Om obscurity. Sit. Sun-dried apricots tango breaths. Common loons settle on a Solarbee island at lake's heart. We lie back to woodpecker poking high in a pinecone-loaded ponderosa erect. Branches reach towards a first-of-the-moon below a waiflike wave cloud lost on a jeweled turquoise sea. Mosquito sucked skin bumps itch like hell. A lizard pumps the sandstone (so many cones to hump it real good under). Monarchs flutter, a companionship of airy bodies, over our thump thumpity heart beats. A bee gets smashed between me and thee. It's going to be a hot day, indeed.

West

The way: matted fishing line, coot carcass, blue glass shards, dead Dr. Pepper can, a white family tan sprawled serene upon a Mexican serape. Faraway canoe floats two on champagne-sun-sparkling waters: a lyrical cast of lines. Nature walk comes to a halt around the rock-strewn dam of the West. Clusters of Mexican sunflowers bend at water's edge, circles on water surface yellow, oh yellow so, orange, a channel of green. Gourd vines stretch arms to concrete curb as if tempted to tangle ankles, to yank us back into morning pulse.

Fragments of Southwestern Youth

Stink beetles balance
beaks
on splintered porch.
Arizona daze,
San Francisco Peaks
sanctify.
Dragonflies flash blue
as jelly shoes.
Chicken-egg scoop
coop.

Sunflowers arch
rock-hunked roads
through ponderosa pine.
Jewelry-maker
neighbor, turquoise nuggets
machine drills, echoes.

Pine bough huts,
Sinagua potsherds,
black-on-white patterns
fragment underfoot;
daydreams dead awaken
earthen palms:
ontological monsoon.

No cell phone, no gps.
Sun out time: time-in
moon orb oozes behind
Mars Hill:

no ears ringing, no calls
from home or to home,
not in far-gone
forest of youth.

Canyon de Chelly Echoes

There is silence. In: silence
There is no silence. In: footsteps, breath, stir of stream, dry breeze dry.
There is sky, blue corn blue. "The sun has been good to us," the Navajo
    woman speaks
softly arched over a host of turquoise turtles & arrowheads & bears &
    juniper seed beads.
There are birds. Up high, an inky raven spellbinds: soars with shadow cast
    on sandstone,
teases red tail hawk into a scream. Pictographs of scorpion & four
    directions on rock face.
There is place. "Over there, crumbling, used to be four stories high,
    Anasazi."
White House Ruins. Tan horse tethered to barbwire fence; a blow of raw
    manure flows.
There are people. Artisan shines silver & stone, Diné jewelry. "I remember
    you,"
recalls the man; his face melds into red stone of cliff walls.
There is history. Black & white photograph. "That's my family here,
shot by Ansel Adams in the 1940's," says the Navajo man at canyon's
    depth.
There is art. "I use acrylic paint. It dries fast," says the painter; his hand
    sweeps
Kokopelli on chosen sandstone slabs beneath sprawl of cottonwood nude.
    "Lasts forever."
There are storytellers. "Pick up the art. Feel how light the rock." Raise to
    winter
sun & it sparkles like the water we crossed to land in this place.

Played the flute down to keep the people happy.

The journey in, the journey out.

Lightning.

Healing hand of Medicine Man.

Journey of Life.

Sun & rain.

The four seasons.

There are visitors. Did we miss it? He nods, "*Aoo`*."
There is moment. Hoof prints stamped into cool sand. Echoes: lost in
wonder, earth & sky.

Visitor at Tsaile Lake

It's dry as drought. A freckle-face cow startles the way, horns point tips to hip. Sun bleached tree limbs strew land all over the place like moo bones. Indian paint brush flame. Grasshoppers buzz the path, streak sand with dot lines, sashaying among piñon pine and juniper to a clearing. Clouds smile wisping turquoise sky, reflecting Tsaile Lake. Horsetails, four, dance lyrical. A pale pony, muscle-legs shades of sage, ignores, mane and tail, ink-black as raven wing shine, tendril a bellowing sky. A pitch-black horse, white splotched down its sides like a painted on saddle, skedaddles. Albino stallion, eyes lined pink, bucks. Hoofs tread coral sand amidst thickets of sea-green sagebrush: itch, itch, I itch, sneeze, wheeze. Wind blows a current to a reddish mare grazing a frenzy feed of native grass. All the wild horses I pass. Folks at lakeshore tug trout while bridal-white pelicans rise, rise. A truck of boys get stuck today–muck spins wheels, stop again, again spin, at lakes end. Navajo women in a pickup pull up, say: "Are you from around here?"

Drip Wish

The woman peers
    out the
        tent screen,
            looking,
        flat
on her backbone,
    at bloat between
monolithic
        slot of volcanic
            tuff
raven appears
    a smear,
wimpled mesh slants
            in a
                draft,
    airplane vapor
trails the violet-
        blue-blue-
    blue vibrant as
finger paint
        there
and gone
    like
        childhood
etch-a-sketch
    lines drawn,
shaken
    evaporate.
Momentarily,
            she squints,
    exhales
        classic bubblegum
wish
    blown
        pop
            bone

Unspoken

sunlight smites
geometric glitz
on anthracite backs
of carpenter bees
whirring nigh a congeries
of blood-orange flowers flexed
sweet from a vine cactus
thrusting
honey-glazed sun

amaranthine skyline
whirlpools behind
the hovering bees
inconstant, illusory,
antediluvian

& God is best
left unspoken for
words dam dreams
& hinder
the beautiful
beautiful flow

Wendy Gist is the author of *Moods of the Dream Fog*. She's had her poetry and prose featured in *Amsterdam Quarterly, Burningword, Glint Literary Journal, Gravel, Grey Sparrow Journal, Juked, Poetry Pacific, The Lake (UK), Oyez Review, Soundings Review, Toad Suck Review, Yellow Medicine Review* and many other fine journals. A native Arizonan, she now lives in New Mexico, where she serves as Co-founding Editor of *Red Savina Review*. Her articles, essays and columns have been seen in leading regional, national and international magazines.